My Parachute Is Beige

THE CUBICLE DWELLER'S GUIDE TO GETTING BY

My Parachute Is Beige

KEN BROWN

ABRAMS IMAGE

NEW YORK

"Success is stumbling from failure to failure without losing your enthusiasm."

—Winston Churchill

INTRODUCTION

This book was made for you, the cube dweller who is perfectly content staying in your dead-end job, as long as there's a paycheck every other week. Think of this book as your primer to staying employed while far more competent workers around you are downsized, belt-tightened, pink-slipped, laid off, let go, severed, found redundant, disengaged, or inactivated.

You don't have to read *My Parachute Is Beige* front to back. Feel free to dip in anywhere. Read some of it or all of it. You might be satisfied by just four or five really good tips and skip the rest. Heck, it doesn't have to be read at all! Half the book is funny pictures.

Best of all, this book isn't going to ask you to "learn" anything new. There are no groundbreaking techniques or resources. This book will never ask you to "think outside the box," rate your SWOT (Strengths, Weaknesses, Opportunities, Threats), or envision where you want to be five years from now. Your current core competency (i.e., collecting a paycheck) doesn't need to expand one iota.

My Parachute Is Beige is the art of keeping your job with utter artlessness and with a total commitment to expending absolutely no effort. The advice is so easy, you could do it in your sleep (i.e., at work). Five years from now? By using this book, you could be doing in five years exactly what you are doing right now. Sound good? Read on.

FROM CRIB TO CUBE

You have been training to sit in an office cube since before you could walk. Really, the only difference between your cozy playpen, with its brightly colored mobiles, and your adult cubicle, with its computer and decorative screen saver, is that you now have to walk down the hall to the rest rooms rather than cutting loose in your diapers. Your primary activity remains the same: Hanging out and taking naps!

ESSENTIALS
of a well-appointed desk

In high school, your worth was measured by the car you drove, the sports you played, and the people you hung out with. In college, the measuring stick moved to more important things such as what you drank and what music you listened to. As an adult, you'll be measured by how much you earn and how much you can afford to pay for a haircut. If you're working in a cubicle, we suggest you keep those details close to your chest. In the workplace, you want to offer some hints to your personality, but not too many. The man in this photograph has a perfect balance of professional and personal. His desk says, "My name is Buddy LaFrance and I like to smoke." 'Nuff said.

BUDDY LaFRANCE

water cooler GOSSIP

Gossip is the highlight of a cubicle dweller's day. Your co-workers are a virtual cable network of opinions, guesses, and so-called reliable sources about who is about to get fired, who just stabbed someone in the back to get a promotion, and who smelled of alcohol. The obvious spots for a coffee klatch are the kitchen, the water cooler, and the hot new employee's cubicle. Enjoy your time there, but to get the real scoop, watch who goes to lunch with the boss's assistant. Your boss's assistant barely acknowledges you, but his lunch buddy might spill the beans over a couple of after-work beers.

LOOK! BUSY

If your boss, or one of his or her minions, is patrolling the halls, you must sit up straight and look busy. Stare at a piece of paper, muttering to yourself, "This can't be right…" Then grab a pile of papers (Excel spreadsheets work best) and march up and down the aisles, not hurriedly, but purposefully, as though you were on your way to somewhere important to discuss something important with some person of importance.

Perfect
your
POKER FACE

The ideal job allows you to simply stand by while a big machine does its thing. You need to be there in case the machine breaks down, but you don't really need to do anything while it's running. Do cultivate a certain hardworking yet cheerful look, with just a hair of grim intensity, so that your bosses will have a good feeling when they walk by.

How to ANSWER the PHONE

Four years of college and no one taught you how to answer the phone in a business setting? Should you answer by announcing your name, your company, your department, or just hello? We say: Less is more. Bark out just your last name and you will command respect. (Or, ideally, confuse the caller so that he or she hangs up and calls someone else.)

SUBTLE, YET EFFECTIVE.

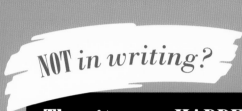

NOT *in writing?*

Then it never HAPPENED.

If you need a favor or are trying to clean up a mistake, follow up your revised e-mail (see page 49, "Accidents Happen") with a stroll down the hall to talk in person, especially if you've got one of those bosses with an "open door" policy. (Personally, we prefer the "closed door" policy: Bosses who are neither seen nor heard are easiest to ignore.) Think of verbal conversation as "erasable." You might even find your boss a bit forgetful, in which case you can get out of a bind by claiming that you'd discussed whatever it was at a previous date. Never try to flip the blame to anyone else, just act befuddled yet understanding.

LEAVE
your lifestyle at
HOME

*Unless your
evenings
and your
w e e k e n d s*
are filled with
nothing more col-
orful than watch-
ing *SportsCenter*, do
not ever talk about your
personal life at work. You
are bound to offend someone.
You just never know. That straight-
looking guy in legal might be a raw food
fanatic. The assistant with the tattoos might
have one on her ass that says "Buns for Jesus."
And who wants to know that the president herself
lets her three dogs sleep in her bed? No one. Really.

E-MAIL *never* FAILS

Calling in sick is so obvious. With e-mail, it's also totally unnecessary. You won't have to hold your nose so you sound stuffed up, and you may not even have to take the day as a PTO (business babble for "paid time off"). Set your alarm for 5:30 A.M., write a quick note to your boss saying that you've been vomiting all night so you're going to try to get some sleep, but that you can check your e-mail and stay "up to speed" from home. Then set your alarm for 10:00 A.M. and go back to sleep. Send an e-mail every two hours and you should be in the clear.

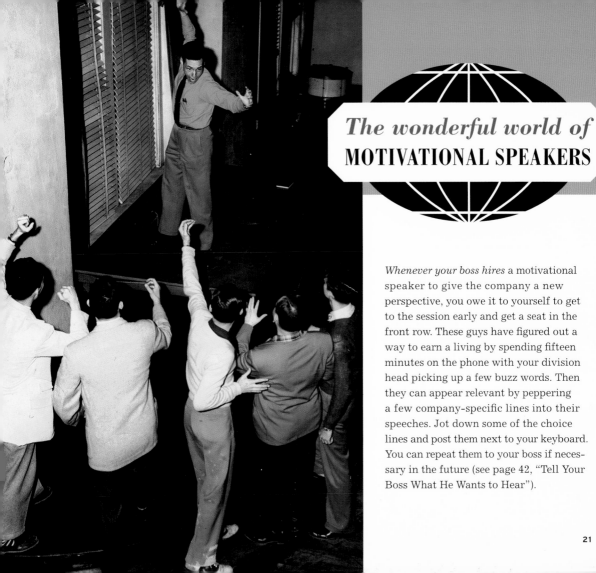

The wonderful world of MOTIVATIONAL SPEAKERS

Whenever your boss hires a motivational speaker to give the company a new perspective, you owe it to yourself to get to the session early and get a seat in the front row. These guys have figured out a way to earn a living by spending fifteen minutes on the phone with your division head picking up a few buzz words. Then they can appear relevant by peppering a few company-specific lines into their speeches. Jot down some of the choice lines and post them next to your keyboard. You can repeat them to your boss if necessary in the future (see page 42, "Tell Your Boss What He Wants to Hear").

copy machine
GO-TO-GAL

One day, copy machines will be obsolete
(God willing). In the meantime, they tend to
be the bane of everyone's existence, breaking down at random. Don't be distraught by
this: Just think of all the blessed time you
will have on your hands trying to "unjam"
the machine. Open all the drawers, check
the slots, shake the toner, and so on.

Before accepting a job, you need to figure out the breadth and the depth of the ass quotient of your future boss. There are untold numbers of miserable people working for George Steinbrenner and Donald Trump who left the interview thinking, "They didn't seem that bad." When interviewing, if the office is quieter than a funeral home and the employees avoid eye contact, you can bet the boss is an ass. If the office has inspirational posters ("If It's Worth Doing, It's Worth Doing WELL!") and the employees seem like they're at a church revival meeting, you can pretty much guarantee the boss is an ass. You're looking for low-level chatter and some milling about, a mellow, shopping mall vibe.

It's *NOT* the size of the ASS on the boss.

It's whether the boss is an ASS.

You may have to build up to this tip, as it takes some finesse. The goal here is to put yourself in the best possible light by finding the two stupidest, least attractive, most socially inept people at your company, and sitting between them in meetings or ad hoc gatherings. Encourage their quirks by providing props such as sticky caramels or pens that are out of ink. You'll radiate intelligence and competence by comparison. It's critical, however, that you appear a bit embarrassed to be there. You don't want anyone to think you chose to sit there, nor, under any circumstances, can you be seen as their friend.

The fine art of FRAMING YOURSELF

Numbers don't kill careers...

People KILL CAREERS.

In any company, it's not your boss you need to fear most, it's those seemingly harmless financial people. These folks love to find "unmet goals" and identify the employees who aren't meeting them. You need to make friends with the financial department. This way you'll know what is going into their quarterly reports and can make that information work for you.

PERFECT ONE SMALL SKILL.

We love voice mail. Record a long outgoing message that identifies you and your position at the company, offers suggestions as to where the caller might redirect his or her phone call, and finally provides your e-mail address in case of further queries. If you're lucky, the caller will hit "0" and be rerouted to someone else. In the worst case, you'll get an e-mail, which is much easier to deal with than a telephone conversation. If the ringing distracts you from your office's quirky decor, set it to go directly to voice mail by dialing into the system and selecting that option.

The BIGGER they are, the HARDER their FALLOUT

Once a year, the Truly Big Guys, investors or senior-level corporate officers from the home office, will show up to appraise your company. These guys with C's after their names (CEO, CFO, COO) are your boss's bosses. You will always know when the Big Guys are coming by the erratic behavior your boss exhibits in the days prior to their arrival. Suddenly your boss will start acting like a boss, giving decisive directions ("Remove that Dilbert poster!") and setting a clear agenda ("Nobody speak unless spoken to, and no gum chewing!"). The question is, other than not chewing gum, what should you do when the Big Guys come calling? That's what sick days are for (see page 20, "E-mail Never Fails").

Remember that episode of Friends when Rachel decides to smoke so that she can hang out with her boss and the cool kids at work? Coffee is today's cigarette, so develop a taste for it. We suggest decaf, however, as the real thing can give you more energy than you really need at work. Preparing and drinking coffee takes time, and you can offer to go out on a coffee run, ideally with the cute intern. A time killer with benefits!

MAPS ARE GOOD
MAPS WITH PINS ARE *Better*

When decorating the walls of your cubicle, it is not a good idea to put up a calendar with holidays and your vacation days circled in red. Posting the office pools for the Oscars or March Madness is only slightly better, as it shows you have some team spirit. Street maps make excellent cubicle adornments. Street maps with pins stuck in certain spots are even better. And street maps with different-colored pins joined by colored string are about as good as it gets. If anyone walks by and asks what's with the map, you can say, "I'm working on something." Stand up and move the pins and string around from time to time. Months later, when you take down the map, if anyone asks what happened to it, you can answer, "I couldn't get the logistics to work."

At least once a year, at the company Holiday Party, you are going to have to party with your co-workers. Do not be misled by the festive decorations or the number of exclamation points on the reminder notices posted by the restrooms and elevators, in the employee lunch room, and in the company newsletter; this is not a time to let your hair down. Do not dance. Do not flirt. Do not drink. Make one beer your limit. After two, you risk admitting to a crush on the sales department assistant. By three or four, you're calling your boss Barf Vader, which is not only job endangering, but not very funny.

IF YOU ACT
LIKE IT'S YOUR
*Retirement
Party*
IT MAY WELL BE

Tell *your* boss what *he* wants to hear

As anyone who has ever written a résumé knows, the facts are there to be manipulated. When your boss asks for a report, whether it be about current market trends, or an analysis of your company's SWOT (Strengths, Weaknesses, Opportunities, Threats), you need to know that he or she is really looking for a collection of a few shady facts and anecdotal conjecture that will support whatever he or she currently believes. So, while your co-workers rush around doing research, gathering data, maybe even cutting into their non-work television time by conducting after-hours focus groups, you need only sit back, figure out what your boss wants to hear, and give him or her exactly that.

LET'S SEE IF THIS ARRANGEMENT WORKS IF WE GIVE THE NEW GUY THAT TINY OFFICE BY THE TRASH ROOM.

The majority of your work time is spent sitting in a chair. How you sit in a chair says a lot about you. You may slouch if you are alone in your cubicle. But be aware of your posture when in a meeting. The proper meeting chair posture is a forty-five degree angle lean, shoulders slightly hunched, with much of your weight pressed on your right forearm and elbow. From this basic position, you should occasionally pick up your pen and take a few notes. What you write is not important. Look up to briefly make eye contact with the speaker, but not so much that he or she will try to engage you. At least twice per meeting, you should gently nod your head, as if agreeing with the last statement. And once per meeting, you should furrow your brow, in a manner that conveys, "I hadn't thought of that!"

How to:

Sit in a chair

The Eyes Never Lie

When speaking with a female co-worker, it is advisable to look her in the eyes and not to stare at her breasts. This is particularly true if the female is your boss. Then again, if your boss asks for ideas or volunteers, look at her breasts, not her eyes. Hopefully, she'll be either too flustered or too disgusted to call on you.

ACCIDENTS HAPPEN:
THE ART OF
Fabricating
Excuses

At some point, you are going to screw up at work. The good news is that you can usually cover your tracks. If your boss loves e-mail more than his or her voice, use your computer to reinvent the past. Did you forget to do something? Send yourself an e-mail that requests a meeting, submits an order, confirms a deadline, or otherwise proves you tried to accomplish what you were supposed to accomplish. Forward it to your boss, changing the sent date to re-create the scenario that best fits your needs. Voilà! You're covered.

accessorized
GOOFING OFF

On days when you just don't have the energy to keep walking in an extended Möbius strip, carrying Excel spreadsheets, acting as if you were working, you can also just stand around and carve valuable minutes out of your work day. The most important factor here is not your posture or what you're wearing, but where you are standing. If you can find a fax machine, printer, scanner, filing cabinet, or an assortment of office supplies, you can eat away a good fifteen to twenty minutes per visit. Standing by the elevator bank, the vending machines, or just staring out a large common window is good for only three to four minutes before suspicion sets in.

ARE YOU PULLING MY THUMB?

+ headphones voice mail

ideal

When you first started working, you probably thought that people wearing headphones were the ultimate dorks. Think again. After the jammed copy machine, there is no greater tool or device to assist you in doing nothing at work than the headphone. Send your calls to voice mail, holster up the headphone, and stare at your wall. Whenever anyone walks by, say things like, "When can it get here? Is that your best price? Uh-huh…uh-huh…that's right…sounds great…yeah, I'll have to get back to you on that…" You should also have a pen and Post-it nearby. If anyone tries to talk to you, hold up one finger and scribble a note—"I'll call you"—while never breaking stride from your "Uh-huh…uh-huh…could you repeat that? Sorry, I had someone in my office."

THINK GLOBALLY

BUT ACT

Lazily

Most companies want to take advantage of opportunities in the international marketplace. People are hired as consultants or trained internally to be the experts on foreign customs, etiquette, and the conversion of the yen. You too could learn a lot from foreign business practices. Rather than focus on the burgeoning giant of China, have a look at Mexico, where they take siestas, or France, where everyone drinks a bottle or two of wine at lunch and then goes home. Expand your horizons!

PULLING YOUR OWN WEIGHT

Bosses love the idea of everyone pulling their own weight. Learn from the carnies, my friends: Their dumbbells were made of styrofoam. It was their slick showmanship, not their brute strength, that impressed the audience. So if you're ever drawn into an important project, remember: It's not the work you do, but the work you look like you're doing. For the next week or so, stay late every night. Send e-mails during the weekend. And, if you sleep in your clothes and show up unwashed, your boss will believe you gave it your all.

THINKING
INSIDE THE
BEAR TRAP

Have you been asked to think outside the box? We suggest you do the exact opposite. Stick to old-school methods and you'll neither excel nor fail. For example, create a situation in which everything takes ten times longer than it should by throwing more clichéd suggestions into the "box." Observations such as "let's take this off-line," "let me do some research and we can revisit this," "I think this really needs to be brought to a committee," and "I hear she's flying below the radar on that one" will help secure your position as an employee who is paying (some) attention but put the kibosh on movement that might require work.

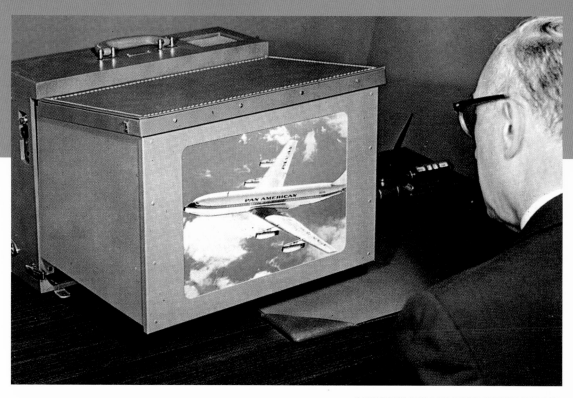

SAM NEVER LIKES TO THINK OUTSIDE THE BOX.

GIVING
appropriate gifts

Eventually someone at work is going to retire, or have a baby, and you're going to have to buy a present. Remember, you're not getting the present just for the recipient, but for all of your co-workers to see and judge. You don't want your gift to stand out. That is key. The gift should show no signs of personality. A tiny T-shirt with the word SINGLE printed on it may be funny to you and me, but a new mother won't like it. An inflatable reindeer, however, works on any occasion.

EXPENSE ACCOUNTS Aren't for the likes of you

The rule as to who pays for a business lunch is a simple one, easily remembered by the mathematical formula VP/P (or, Vice President over Peon). The person with the highest-ranking title picks up the bill. You'll want to avoid paying a bill at all costs when out with superiors, as it will draw attention to you, and it will actually be money out of your own pocket. In fact, you shouldn't be going out to lunch with superiors at all. Leave that to your corporate-ladder-climbing buddies.

make use of the
SMILE & NOD

the lost art of
SHAKING HANDS

In our modern era, you are likely to receive an e-mail from the person sitting in the next cubicle, telling you that the 11:00 A.M. meeting has moved to 11:30 A.M., to which you respond, "Fine," to which they respond, "Great. See you then!" There is no place for the firm but friendly handshake in this world. Or is there? Shake the hands of your boss and co-workers when you're saying hello or good-bye. For one thing, it takes time and encourages idle chitchat. And you've made a good impression while conserving brainpower.

dare to be the CLOWN

In these present times of cutbacks, down-sizing, belt-tightening (i.e., firing people), your bosses don't just look at competence or achievement. They also think about team morale. If your bosses care about how their best employees will react to losing colleagues and absorbing a bigger work load, they can be influenced by your internal role as the beloved buddy of the best employees. If you have carefully cultivated the role by which you make everyone else feel better about his or her own skills and self-worth, you may well survive in spite of your obvious expendability.

SECRET SANTA
holiday gift swap

Why do the people in human resources insist on holding a Secret Santa/Holiday Gift Swap, where each employee draws the name of a fellow worker to whom he or she will give an inexpensive (read: useless) present? Avoid this little ritual at all costs. Make sure you are away from your cube when the hat o' names comes around. Feign sickness on the day actual swappage occurs. Your boss won't be there either. This is one for the middle-aged women of accounts payable.

Resist the urge to
GO BEYOND

THE COMPANY NEWSLETTER

If your company has a newsletter, you will need to develop the skill to be mentioned the right number of times (roughly once every eighteen months) for the right reason (nothing that calls too much attention to you as an individual). Any less notice and your boss may ask the embarrassing question, "And how long have you been with us?" Any more and you risk being considered a suck-up by your co-workers, or worse—someone worth watching by your boss.

SAY YES to GYPSY ADVICE

Your human resources department is not good for much more than information on benefits. (And even that is questionable.) If you really want advice about your career, go see a gypsy. She'll tell you the truth, as she has no stake in your life. Plus, she'll never give you a test that says you should have been a music teacher.

EXHIBIT
mild enthusiasm

She whom you must obey

In every company, there is always one person who knows how to get things done. He or she seems to have worked at the company since shortly after the earth cooled. She knows every back door and trick in the book to get around the system, avoiding red tape, copies in triplicate, and any "team building" exercises. You need to figure out who this person is. You need to befriend her. Telltale signs: The boss will jokingly say things like, "I work for Helen," pretending to be self-effacing when, in fact, in spite of job title, salary, and retirement package, he or she does work for Helen.

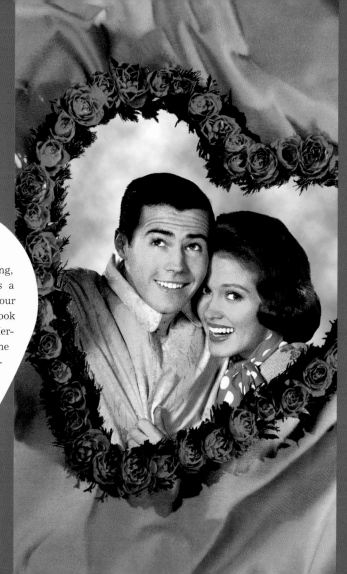

Office Romance

No matter how discreet you think you're being, becoming romantically involved on the job is a surefire way to draw attention to yourself. Your co-workers have nothing better to do than to look for telltale signs and fire up the rumor mill. A Hershey's Kiss left on a desk, leaving for lunch at the same time, even a glance on the way to the copier, can all be used to confirm their suspicions. Then it's only a matter of time before human resources calls you both in, and your boss starts noticing you because your new friend really is someone "up-and-coming" and no one can figure out what he or she sees in you.

WATCH OUT, THIS COULD BE YOU.

ALL WORKPLACES HAVE
Uniforms

While it is more obvious in a hospital operating room or at Burger King, all workplaces have uniforms. You need to assess if business casual means khaki pants with or without side cargo pockets. Can you get away with an open checked shirt? Only with a pipe and slippers to complete the look, and only if your co-workers dress similarly. Your goal is to fit squarely in the middle of what everyone else is wearing. If that means flowered Hawaiian shirts, so be it.

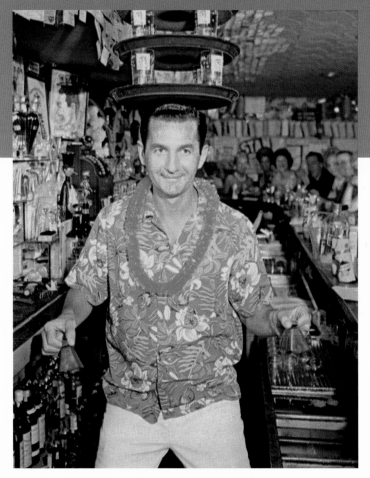

IF YOU LIVE IN HAWAII, CASUAL FRIDAY IS ALOHA FRIDAY.

Candy Collection

Stopping off on the way to work to pick up bagels or an assortment of chocolates is a good way to ingratiate yourself with your co-workers and improve morale (see page 64, "Dare to Be the Clown"). It's important, however, that you avoid announcing, "I brought in coconut patties and fruit cream ruffles! They're in the kitchen." You need to be seen putting out the candy by a third party. This way, every time someone asks, "Who brought the fruit cream ruffles?" your personal publicist can reveal the source. The other, more important rule is, bring enough for everyone.

MINIATURE COCONUT PATTIES

Shenandoah Candies ... The Candy of Florida

PECAN ROLL

SHENANDOAH DOUBLE FEATURE

Southern Sweets

CHOCOLATES

...h Candies ... The Candy of Florida

SHENANDOAH CANDIES, INC.   MIAMI, FLA.

Four Fruit Cream Puffies

SHENANDOAH CANDIES, INC.   MIAMI, FLA.

Southern Sweets by Shenandoah

SHENANDOAH CANDIES BY H. X. WOMACK, INC.   MIAMI, FLA.

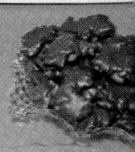

GOD
is in the details

Your boss may play at paying attention to the details, but the fact is, your boss didn't get to where he or she is by sweating the small stuff. Still, you'll discover one small detail, generally of no significance, that your boss will roll out to maintain the illusion. Your job is to remember that detail and to never do anything to contradict it. If his story is about the time he switched the company from using white glossy mailing tubes to plain brown mailing tubes, thus saving thousands of dollars, never use white glossy tubes in front of him.

Surviving role-playing at the *OFF-SITE WORKSHOP*

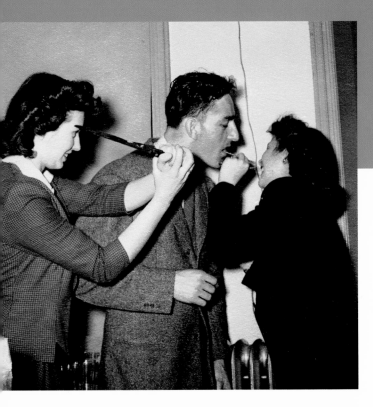

Who is to blame for the intersection of role-playing and business? Tom Peters? Many companies have bought into the idea. Try to survive the event with the least personal humiliation or degradation. Like Aleksandr Solzhenitsyn, who survived eight years in a Soviet gulag, and Nelson Mandela, who kept his chin up during twenty-seven years in a South African prison, you will most likely make it through this retreat. Like them, you might even write the definitive memoir of your ordeal. (Or at least an e-mail.) The key is to remember to hang onto your essential self.

LISA IS TOP BANANA, BETTY IS OUR TOMATO.

Never offer a heartfelt opinion at work; rather, footnote the opinions of others. Start out each day reading the Yahoo home page. In ten minutes or less, you can get sufficiently informed about the latest wars, natural disasters, Paris Hilton, or Barack Obama to feign conversant knowledge of the world. If your co-workers are chatting about current events, don't confront or contradict what's already been said. Keep your points short. Along those same lines, keep your behavior in line with that of your peers. If the girls want to perform at the company talent show, ask to be included in the most banal choreography, and never, never take a solo. Keep your attire similar, and soon no one will be able to tell you apart. And they're not going to fire all four of you!

when in
DRONE

How to:
SURVIVE COMPETITION

Even when your career goals are no higher than to not get noticed and to not get fired, there's always someone younger, dumber, and more willing to do nothing for less. To compete in the new marketplace, you need to focus on those jobs where the company will look last when considering an upgrade. Like so many success stories, yours too could start in the mailroom. Unlike the heroes of Horatio Alger's stories, your dream is to stay there.

A LITTLE
Company Logo
GOES A LONG WAY

If your company has its logo emblazoned on sweatshirts, pens, stationery, canvas bags, and more, don't go overboard with the free advertising. Even the president of the United States wears only a discreet pin of the American flag on his lapel. You don't want to look like the head coach of an NFL team until they pay you like the head coach of an NFL team.

Team Building

When your company decides to run a "team-building session," look to the real teams for advice. Sports teams have so-called bench warmers. These are the guys who sit on the bench without much chance of seeing action. That's your goal. As soon as your "team" is assembled, volunteer to take notes. The note-taker cannot be expected to participate fully, as you'll be too busy getting it all down.

JUST GRIN AND BEAR IT.

90

There's no U in "team" either

Spinners of sports clichés are fond of saying, "There's no 'i' in team." Look around at your co-workers the next time your floor has a fire drill. Is this a "team" you are psyched to be a part of? Or do most of them look like they were the kids picked last for dodge ball in seventh-grade gym? In fact, look really closely. If you were on a deserted island, would you want any of them on the island with you? "U" need to figure out a way to go undrafted by this team or, if chosen, how to get on the injured reserve list pronto.

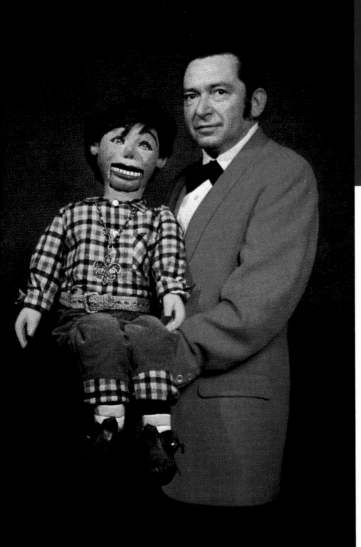

PRESENTATIONS (ARE) FOR DUMMIES

If you make a presentation, you're going to look like a dummy. We promise. You may have mastered the art of PowerPoint, but no one ever comes across as smart, clever, or amusing when making a presentation. If you were the boss, people would rush up to tell you how great/ helpful/informative you were. But you're not the boss. And if you ever even think twice about saying no to a presentation, remember that bosses always want follow-up after any presentation. If you cannot get out of a presentation, you must quit.

IF THEY CAN'T FIND YOU, THEY CAN'T FIRE YOU.

That's all folks!

Acknowledgments

I offer my profound respect and gratitude (and sympathy) to Michael Murphy, the original cubicle dweller. The book was his original idea, and it was through a unique collaboration, plundering my extensive ephemera archive and adding his insightful observations, that we have come up with the indispensable tome you now hold. Michael and I would both like to acknowledge the invaluable guidance of Ann Treistman, our editor at Harry N. Abrams, who hunkered down in the paper-strewn trenches, poring over postcards and snapshots, and who continuously kept all the various parts and personalities moving forward toward the goal of turning the parts into a whole book. We would also like to give special thanks to Alissa Faden, whose crackerjack design skills have elevated this project all the way.

–KEN BROWN

Editor: Ann Treistman
Designer: Alissa Faden
Production Manager: MacAdam Smith

Library of Congress Cataloging-in-Publication Data
Brown, Ken, 1944–
  My parachute is beige : the cubicle dweller's guide to getting by / by Ken Brown.
    p. cm.
  ISBN-13: 978-0-8109-9539-0
  ISBN-10: 0-8109-9539-5
  1. Work—Humor. 2. Offices—Humor. I. Title.
  PN6231.W644B76 2008
  650.02'07—dc22

                          2007030678

Text copyright © 2008 Ken Brown
Illustrations/photographs copyright © 2008 Ken Brown
Icon graphics by Alissa Faden
Cover image courtesy of the New York Public Library

Published in 2008 by Abrams Image, an imprint of Harry N. Abrams, Inc.

Printed and bound in China
10 9 8 7 6 5 4 3 2 1

HNA
harry n. abrams, inc.
a subsidiary of La Martinière Groupe

115 West 18th Street
New York, NY 10011
www.hnabooks.com